If we <u>really</u> want, we can all be peaceful.

This copy of Peace Is Within Our Reach was printed through the loving generosity of the Integral Yoga® Institutes of California as a grateful offering to Sri Swami Satchidananda and the cause of peace everywhere.

Peace
is within
our
reach

*Excerpts from talks
by Sri Swami Satchidananda*

Integral Yoga® Publications • Yogaville, Virginia

Library of Congress Cataloging in Publication Data:
Satchidananda, Swami.
  Peace is within our reach.
  1. Peace—Religious aspects. I. Title.
  BL65.P4S27 1985   294.5'17873   85-14384
ISBN 0-932040-29-2

Integral Yoga® Publications
Satchidananda Ashram—Yogaville
Route 1 Box 172, Buckingham, Virginia 23921

Peace is closer to us than we can possibly imagine. It is our birthright, an inheritance form our Heavenly Father. Our very nature is peace, just as His nature is peace. It is within and without, in front and behind, above and below, on all sides of us. It can be experienced, if we just open our hearts.

This book is dedicated to that Supreme Peace, and to beings everywhere who are seeking to experience it in their lives. May we all realize that peace within soon, so that the entire creation may be filled with Peace and Joy, Love and Light. May the thoughts expressed in this book help open our eyes to that possibility.

Introduction

A short while ago I was in a disarmament conference in New York City. All the clergy of various faiths had gathered there at the Cathedral of St. John the Divine. There were about twenty-five different religious representatives from all over the globe: Japanese monks, Tibetan monks, Hindu monks, Buddhists, Catholics, Protestants, Sufis, Native Americans. Even people who do not bother much about religion were there also. It was a beautiful gathering of all varieties of people, young and old. There were several thousand gathered in that church. That is the largest cathedral in the world, as many of you might know. Of course, as usual, the television cameras were moving around. They were interviewing many of the participants. One of the reporters came up and pointed a microphone at me.

She asked, "What do you think of this nuclear threat, Swami?" I said, "I love it."

"What? Do you know why we are gathered here?"

"I know it, yes."

"And you say you love it?"

"Yes."

"You must be crazy. How could you possibly say you love it?"

"Because it is this nuclear threat that has brought us together here. We have forgotten all our differences."

Yes, we were all sitting together along the center aisle. A Jain monk, a Benedictine—Brother David Steindl-Rast was there with me—bishops, ministers, all on one side. Across from us were rows of Japanese monks, Tibetan lamas. Normally one would rarely see such a gathering. If by any chance a group like this met, they would be claiming superiority over each other and pulling each other's beards. But here we were all together—not only sitting together, but shaking hands, talking, praying, hugging. It was a blissful gathering that day. So I told the reporter, "If this is the result of a nuclear threat, may it happen more often. Adversities are blessings in disguise. I think God purposely created this threat to bring us together."

It happens over and over again throughout history. For example, at one time there were a lot of factions in a certain country. They could not even form a government. Then a powerful neighboring country started to invade the one with so many factions. The minute the invasion came, the whole of that country became one. The people forgot all their differences. They stood side by side to face the situation, and they won the war. If such crises did not happen, we would not rise above our petty quarrels and come together. Everything is planned by God. When to bring the children together, how to bring the children together— and even when to leave them a long rope to fight and kill each other.

It is true. If God did not want war, it would not be difficult for Him (or Her if you prefer to put it that way) just to think, "No war," and finish it. That's all. God does not have to do anything much. All it would take is simply a thought. Because He said, "Let there be light," light came. Is it not so? "Let there be peace"— wouldn't that be enough if it came from God? Instead of that, why does He say, "Let there be a nuclear threat."? It is easy to go and kneel in front of the altar and say, "Lord, it is all Thy will, it is all for good. You are all merciful, all powerful. You are the doer of everything." It is easy to *say* that, but do we act as if we believe it when we come outside? If you really mean that, who is the cause behind this threat? If He did not like these things cropping up in the world, He could have simply taken away the breath of some people. If He has that capacity, why should He allow these crises? Has He fallen asleep somewhere?

Everything has a purpose in this world. Everybody, everything. Whether it is in an individual, a family, a nation or the whole world, you see this continuously. That is why, in a way, nothing is a miracle to a person who really knows that there is an unseen hand at work. When you do not know that, then you might say, "How could this happen? It must be a miracle." What is impossible to God? Nothing. This is the message that we should be getting by living in this world; the universe-ity should teach us this lesson.

God seems to be saying, "Well, I have given them light, health, peace, and other natural gifts. Everything I gave to them freely, but they do not seem to appreciate these free gifts. They waste them, misuse them, fight over them. Let them suffer for their mistakes and that way learn the truth and regain the peace and harmony. In the form of their conscience, I keep on advising them. And of course I have given them their free choice. If they use it correctly, they will find joy in life. If not, they suffer."

So let us see. Maybe something nice will come out of all of this. If a nuclear war comes, there will be no winner. Everybody will be losers. In fact, there will not even be any losers. No winners and no losers: complete annihilation. Let us set aside our egoistic, selfish nature. The only things that can help us are faith in God, sincere prayer, love for one another, and harmonious living.

Contents

PEACE

Non-violence

If everyone would just make up their minds to be kind and gentle and loving at all times, in all ways, then one day the word "violence" would be taken out of the dictionary. We can make that happen. Let us not expect some great person to come and do it for us. Each one of us has the capacity, and the responsibility, to do it. It would be enough if each individual would decide today: "In my own life, I will take a vow of *ahimsa*, non-violence. In every way possible, I will stay away from causing pain to anybody or anything." Good things catch on quickly; within a week you would see this decision growing tenfold. Please remember this and do what you can.

If each one led a peaceful life, would we not have a peaceful world? Let your own life be an example. In recent years—the '60s, '70s and '80s particularly—there have been so many peace marches and demonstrations. Yet many of them ended up in violence. Why? If we begin with peace, should we not expect to end up with peace also? If the intended peaceful demonstration becomes violent, it means that those demonstrators did not have the capacity to retain tranquility. Then, any trifling thing is enough to disturb that peace. Even though there was a heartfelt desire for peace, there was also a built-up hatred against the police and other authorities. Yet those authorities are simply doing their work. Nothing can happen without orderliness, without discipline, and they are trying to maintain order. If you get disturbed the minute you see them, you will have lost your peace.

Sometimes we hear the argument that someone who has done violence to another person should be punished. Even then we have no right to punish anyone; on the other hand, we should *educate* that person. Sending a person to prison is not done as punishment. That is why we call the facilities "correctional institutions." We try to correct the people who commit crimes, because in a way they are sick both physically and mentally. They make mistakes because of the disease in their minds. We sometimes make a plea for "temporary insanity"; but is there actually any crime where you could not make that plea? Would a sane person ever kill another, rob another, injure another? No. Every crime committed is done in a state of "temporary insanity." Crime itself is an insane act. Instead of condemning the criminals, we should love them and try to correct them; help them to become better people. That is what a religious person would do, a person who believes in God.

A violent act can never put down another violent act. If you do not believe in violence, you should not exhibit violence in any way. Every act of yours must be based on non-violence. That means you have to build up that capacity within yourself, that faith in the virtue of non-violence. Until that capacity is developed peace marches, demonstrations, protests and things like that will not bring any real benefit. It would be better for you to sit still and find peace within yourself; then you will be able to take peaceful thoughts, peaceful vibrations, with you wherever you go.

Here is an example: If you really feel that certain government expenditures are not right, and you don't want to be a part of it, you have the liberty to say, "I cannot support these things." That means you refuse to pay the taxes. Of course there will be consequences, and you should be ready to face them lovingly. Mahatma Gandhi had his Salt *Satyagraha*. He violated the law in a way, and he knew what the consequences would be. He was willing to take those consequences, so he expressed his disagreement in that way. Likewise, if you think that they are unnecessarily spending money on various things that are not beneficial, you can say no. But before you say no you should make sure that you are right in saying that. Sometimes what you think of as unnecessary may be needed for the good of the country. You have to be totally sure. You should not think, "Oh, I don't want to give so I'll find some excuse." See if it is for the common welfare of the entire country. Of course, it is even better to think of the welfare of the whole world. But in this case we are talking about the country, because that is who takes the taxes from you. You have to be totally impartial in thinking about it.

You may say, "We have to have arms control." But there is another big group saying, "Because we are weak in weapons, the other people are taking the upper hand. It prevents us from being able to persuade them to talk peace. We have to make ourselves strong first, and then talk peace." In such a case, you have to find out who is right. The international situation is very difficult to understand these days. There is a delicate balance of powers. It is important that nothing weaken us. You may hesitate to spend a little money for something to make yourself strong; but if you are weak and somebody comes and takes over, then you might lose everything. It is hard to make decisions like that as an individual. You should have the complete, overall picture.

In one sense I would even have to agree that we need nuclear arms – and, yes, we also need to talk peace. We need to let the others know that we are at least equally strong. Otherwise our words won't even carry weight. Suppose that you are coming to attack me. I might look at you and say, "Well, I believe in nonviolence so I don't want to return it to you." But you will know whether I am saying it because I believe in *ahimsa* or because I am weak. If I am strong I can even say it more boldly, "I have more strength than you. If I allow my fist to come up against your jaw, all your teeth will be knocked out. One punch is enough. Do you know that? But I believe in *ahimsa*. I don't want to use that strength against you." That is why Gandhiji said, "*Ahimsa* is not for weaklings. You should be strong, and then not cause violence."

At the same time, let us not forget that in the case of nuclear war there will be no winner or loser. There would be total annihilation. Even without war, there is danger of mistakes – with weapons getting into the wrong hands, radioactive waste, and so on. The best solution is to have a heart-to-heart talk with everybody and stop this nonsense.

In most of the cases, our lives are filled with violence. We kill to eat; we kill to dress (furs, leather, etc.); we kill to beautify; we kill to find medicine to save us; we kill in the name of sport or fun; we kill to rob; we kill to rape; we kill to have sex; we kill for scientific research; we kill because of insanity; we kill nature by polluting it just to make some money; we kill to get more territory; we kill just to prove we are strong; we kill to compete; we kill to abort a baby.

The list goes on and on with many more reasons to kill. Where will all this end? All the accumulated *karmas* will certainly kill us in turn. That is why the germs kill us, the toxins kill us, the cancer kills us, the worry kills us, the fear kills us, the accidents kill us, the smog kills us, our own hearts kill us. . . .

What we kill, kills us.

What we eat, eats us.

Peace

Before you get involved in a peace movement, you must have peace yourself. What is the purpose of joining a peace movement? To bring peace to others. In order to bring peace to others, you must carry peace with you into the movement. If you do not have peace, how can you bring peace to others?

You should not try to help others if you yourself need help. Analyze yourself, "What makes me shaky? In what way can I make myself steady, strong?" Help yourself first. Establish yourself. Only a person who has steadied his or her own life will be able to help another. When you are slipping on the road, how are you going to lend a hand to another person who is slipping? You both will fall. So stand steadily, and then lend a hand. Learn to swim before you go to rescue someone who is drowning.

If you were walking on the road and you saw a house on fire, what would you do? You would not go up to the burning house without anything in your hand. You would look for a bucket and some water or something to throw on the fire. You have to equip yourself first in order to put out a fire. Suppose you had a gallon of gasoline in your hand. Would you throw it on the fire? Likewise, if you want to stop violence, what should you have in your hand? Should you take more fuel? No. You must have peace. Without having peace yourself, how are you going to make peace with others? You will just be throwing gasoline on the fire. Probably our peace talks have been failing because we do not have peace ourselves. Peace must be cultivated within; individuals make communities, communities make countries and countries make up our world.

If the world is filled with suffering and killing and insanity, what else can you do but be compassionate and loving? Do you want to become insane yourself? Do you want to go out and kill? No. At least remove yourself from the insanity, and make the part of the world that you occupy a little more peaceful.

If you become peaceful, you will not be disturbed by the world. I do not say that the world will not have problems—there will be disturbances in the world, but you will not be disturbed by them. The world is the world, after all. As far as you are concerned, just be peaceful. Then, even if there is restlessness outside, you will be able to see it peacefully and do what you can to help without disturbing your own peace. A surgeon cannot operate with a shaking hand. First become established in peace yourself, and then operate in the world.

Where is that internal peace we speak about? It is within the mind, is it not? The world is your own projection. If you find peace within you, you will see a peaceful world outside. If you find peace, then you will even know the meaning of all these changes and problems. There cannot be one hundred percent peace all over the world at any given moment. It has never happened that way. The world is a kind of factory. There will never be finished cars all over Detroit. Finished cars may come out and go on their way, but there are many more unfinished cars on the line. In the same way, the world is a kind of factory where we learn to find the peace within. If you find the peace within, you will walk in the world peacefully, and those who are ready will recognize that and come to you to find the way. Those who are not ready will not even come to you. Sometimes they may even laugh at you. Not everybody will have that vision immediately, but everybody will slowly get it in time. All the children will ultimately grow up. The child that is crawling today will be winning the gold medal in the Olympic race of tomorrow. Because I am running in the race today, I should not criticize the crawling baby. Who knows, tomorrow when that baby is running the race I might even be crawling. So we should just allow them to grow. We do not need to hurry them.

The factory will remain a factory; people will continue to pass through, getting polished. Those who are polished and ready for service will go into the showroom. That is what you call a heaven on earth. The earth is still a factory, but the showroom is a heavenly place where the finished products are. Those who are ready look for their service and are helped to go on their journey. Without that help they cannot reach their destination.

First gain peace yourself, and then share it with others through your movements. Prepare yourself for that. A peace movement is a kind of orchestra, a peace orchestra where peaceful music is played. If peaceless people join, then the orchestra will be out of tune and will go to pieces.

Not only do you need to be peaceful to spread peace, but if you lose your peace in the midst of chaos, are you not adding to the chaos? In what way are you helping? At least for the sake of not aggravating the situation, just be peaceful. If nothing else, at least you get the immediate benefit of not adding more chaos to the situation. That is the immediate result. Then, if you are peaceful enough to think, you might even find a solution to the problem. By losing your peace, you are never going to help the situation. Do not be affected by the situation outside. There will always be problems. They are a test for you. Even the nuclear threat is a test for sane people. It makes one think. It makes you reach out to shake hands with someone. Do not think that we went into space to shake hands out of real love and affection. It was not out of comradeship, but out of fear. So you see, chaotic situations force us to find some solution. To reach out and make friends. In that sense, they are a blessing in disguise.

Being peaceful or non-violent does not mean that if you see smoke, you ignore it. If we see a little smoke, certainly there will soon be a big fire somewhere if we do not prevent it. For that purpose, everybody has a right to do something, whatever he or she can. But in the name of prevention we should not create more problems. That is what was happening during the Viet Nam period on many campuses. There were a lot of riots and similar incidents. I happened to be there when such things were happening in one or two places, and this is what I told the students: "You don't want a war there, but what are you doing here? Creating a war. If you don't want violence in that place, how can you cause violence in this one? You are contradicting yourselves."

There is a passive way of doing things, a peaceful way. When we talk about peace, everything about us should be peaceful. Even our actions should be peaceful. We may not get the result we want immediately. It might take some time and it might take some sacrifice, but that does not matter. It is far better than sacrificing your life in the name of violence. All the people who have the capacity should talk about it, think about it, do something to prevent future catastrophes. But in the process we should not create new catastrophes.

If we want peace, we cannot constantly talk about others as our enemies. As long as you treat another group as your enemy, you will never find peace. If you want peace, bring friendship. Even people who do wrong things should not be treated as enemies. They should be approached with compassion and friendliness. If somebody wants to be your enemy, you should not allow it. Instead, you should say, "My God, how can you be my enemy? I don't believe that. You cannot be my enemy because I love you. You are my friend." By putting out positive thoughts, you can even make that enemy into a friend. On the other hand, if someone is a friend and you keep calling him or her your enemy, that is what your friend will become.

There is no power higher than love. Hatred breeds hatred, violence breeds violence. If we sincerely want peace, we have to depend on our soul force, not on anything else.

That is what the great Mahatma Gandhi called "*satyagraha*": trusting in the ultimate truth, which is God. You trust in God and go forth. You do not trust in your fist. It is very hard to do this, but there is no other way. Gandhiji was a great example of this principle. He took time to train his volunteers to be peaceful activists. When they were struck with clubs by the police they never shouted insults. They shouted "Ram!"—a name of God—and accepted the beatings. Gandhiji disagreed with many of the things the British rulers were doing, but he never hated them. He never called a policeman a "pig." Instead, he would say to the officer, "My dear brother, you are the image of God. You are doing your duty; I am doing my duty. Let us love each other. If you want to hit me, do it. That is part of your duty. My duty is to accept that because I believe in soul power; I believe in God." It was a passive form of disagreement. Ultimately, he achieved liberation for the entire country that way.

Only by leading a spiritual life can we bring certain good changes into the political field. A person who is really interested in spiritual life will never resort to violence in order to change anything political. The approach has to be non-violent; it cannot be otherwise.

We should follow Gandhiji's example and never hate the people who wage wars; we should love them. We may not appreciate their actions, and we have every liberty to stop them from acting that way. Still we should love them. When a student makes a mistake, the teacher corrects the student out of love. Even God corrects us in this way. If people are dissatisfied with the political setup or with those who are ruling the country, naturally they should express their dissatisfaction and do something to change the situation. It has happened all over, during every period of history. I feel personally that it is always better to express dissatisfaction in a passive way, rather than attempting to achieve one's ends through violence. Anything achieved through violence will not last long; it will leave an enemy sitting somewhere, plotting against you. If, instead, you make a friend, you need not be afraid of the other person; and he or she need not be afraid of you. The tension will not be there. Permanent peace can never be achieved by violent methods.

POWER

Nuclear Power

Very often I am asked about nuclear power plant meltdowns. I say you do not need to be afraid of a meltdown. It is not going to happen. You can live comfortably and feel safe. Do not melt yourself down thinking of that meltdown. Do not always think of calamities. Make sure that by your present deeds you don't cause them to happen. What you sow now, you reap later.

Do you remember how they talked for months and months about Skylab's falling? Every newscast, every hour. Do you know how many journalists were disappointed because it did not fall on anyone? They could not write a big story about it. It simply fell down one day and that was the end of it. There was no more news about it. But if it had fallen on some important city or on some people, the excitement would have gone on for at least six months. There would have been all kinds of agitation: demonstrations, law suits, insurance claims, and this and that. Even before it fell down they were talking about the possibility of these things. That is the real problem. There is too much anticipation; there are too many preconceived ideas.

So let us not worry about the future too much. Right now there is nothing melting down. If it never happens, you will have melted yourself for nothing. Do not waste your time on these things. We only speak about radioactive meltdown. Why? The whole earth could melt down at any moment. It is true. The sun is coming closer and closer and closer. The whole earth could disappear into a black hole at any time. There is danger of the nuclear winter. Yet, we are still putting up buildings, mowing our lawns, planting vegetables. Do not worry about the future at all. It is just wasted energy. Think of the golden present. "I am here alive today. Let me do the right kind of actions, actions which would not create the wrong future. Let me enjoy the day well. Let me be useful. Let me be peaceful. Let me be easeful." That is the attitude we should all have. Even if you find out that you are going to die the next minute, you should make that minute count. You should feel, "In that case I should act fast; I should do something good right away." You will be the happiest person in the world if you are doing something worthwhile at the moment you die.

If ultimately the bomb does drop, I will take it as God's will. What else can I do if it happens? But as long as it hasn't happened, if it is within our capacity to do something, we should do it. After that, if it has to happen and it does happen, I'll say, "Well, then that was the will of God. Everything we tried failed. It was beyond our human capacity. If He wanted things to be different, He could have prevented it."

This attitude doesn't mean that we should not try to stop these things. We should try in whatever way we can to prevent disaster.

The spread of nuclear power is really a big dilemma now. What we need is the proper understanding. We should think, why do we want nuclear power? What are we doing with it? Most of it goes to make arms and ammunition, is it not so? But if we learn to feel the spiritual oneness by seeing the same spirit in each other, to love each other, we will not need nuclear arms. That is why we are building the LOTUS – Light Of Truth Universal Shrine.

We call ourselves great powers, big powers, superpowers. What is the sign of that super power? Sitting in a concrete cave and putting a finger right on the button, waiting for somebody to say to press it? Our lives are dangling. That is not really the mark of civilization or advancement. We should be living fearlessly, joyfully. We should be able to walk around unarmed, day or night, without even so much as a penknife in the pocket. If you drop something on the road, nobody should steal it; it should go directly to the "lost and found" office.

16

You know, Japan was like that once. When I visited Japan in 1959, I saw that. Their yen did not say, "In God we trust", but they lived a religious life. If you dropped anything on the road and it had an address on it, it would reach you by the next day. If not, you could simply go to the lost and found at the police station. It would be there waiting for you. The buses did not have a conductor to collect your money. You would simply put the fare in the box and take a seat. If you did not have the exact amount, you could put your money in and take the proper change. There was just an open box there. I saw it. People trusted each other. If you were rushing to the railway station and did not have time to buy a ticket, you could just get on the train. When you got off, you would simply walk to the ticket counter and say, "I got on at such-and-such place. Could you please tell me what I owe?"

That is what you call living religion. Religion is not just what happens inside a church or synagogue. Religion is a way of life. It is built on certain principles. When that morality disappears from life, all the problems come. The wars, the nuclear threat, all these things stem from the same cause. We are trying to depend on arms and ammunition to save us. But is it working? The race still goes on. You say, "Because they are stockpiling, we have to do it too." At the same time they are saying, "Because *you* are piling up arms, *we* have to do it." Where will it end? Somebody should be bold enough to come forward with fearlessness and say, "All right. We are going to trust you completely. We will not make any more weapons, and we will never offensively use what we already have." But both sides continue to increase their weapons. Most of our scientific research is going toward this purpose.

The effect goes even deeper than this. When a country makes money by selling arms and ammunition, what kind of vibration does that money bring?

We should think about it. Money earned from selling weapons comes out of violence. The countries who do this are selling things to create more violence. When that money comes into a country, it brings violence with it. It is not well-earned money. Money alone is not important. How it is gotten is more important. You would be far

17

happier with a little money properly earned—even if it were just a few hundred dollars—than you would be with a million dollars ill-earned. Can you disagree with this?

Of course another problem is that the world has a shortage of energy so we think that we must have nuclear power plants. That idea is based on a wrong assumption. We do not have a shortage of energy. We would have more than enough energy for everything we need, if only we would not waste it. We waste a lot. There are millions of electric lights burning day and night without even a switch to turn them off. We continuously create more demand. If we keep on wasting, we will keep on wanting. Even at that, if all the power plants were producing enough to satisfy our present life, somebody would invent some more uses for it and we would still have a shortage. There is such a waste of energy.

Naturally, Mother Nature is really teaching us a good lesson, "You have been wasting what I have given you. Now you will have to go without for a while." We may say, "We are a powerful country." But when another country closes the oil taps there, we freeze here. So my answer to these problems would be, "Learn to live with what you have." Budget your life according to whatever you have—energy, money, food, everything. Do not budget beyond your earning capacity. You should be thinking of income first, and then expenditure; not expenditure first and then income. As soon as you add more expenses, you will want more money. You will be striking. And yet, the more you get, the more you spend. There will never be enough if we live that way. Contentment is golden. If we learn to conserve our energy, we will have plenty. Of course, we keep finding other ways around the problem. Now I have heard that there is more money being allotted for the development of synthetic fuel. It is a good sign, no doubt. But are we going to be happy with that? We may produce synthetic fuel, but there will still be a shortage if we waste it. Let us learn to reduce our wants, or there will be no end to the demand, and no supply will ever be able to fulfill it. There is a proverb, "Waste not, want not." I would say instead, "Want not, waste not." By wanting, wanting, wanting, you are wasting your very life.

18

Our defenses should be controlled by the right people; they should not get caught in the wrong hands. That is the danger of having these modern arms and ammunition. Of course we know the danger in it, but still that is the situation we are in now. The others have a nuclear arsenal, so we feel that we must have one too. Fine. But it is not enough to simply stockpile arms. At the same time we should do whatever is necessary to get us out of the danger. We should go, meet people, talk to people. In fact, I have even thought that if someone would come forward to sponsor it, I would like to gather children from all of the countries in the world, a group of children of all different colors and hues—about two or three from each country—and put them all in a chartered plane, taking them to meet all of the leaders who are causing all the problems. I would not say anything to the leaders except for one thing: "The children want to meet you." I would get an appointment with the president of every country, and then let the children go to them and say, "Father, Mother, please don't kill us." They could stand around and cry a little and that would be the end of the meeting. Then they could go on to some other president. That would really melt the hearts of all these "heads."

We should have face-to-face talks, but in the proper way. We should find some way to show that we trust each other. Of course, just because we have trust, that does not mean we should be weak. But we should be willing to talk genuinely heart-to-heart.

We cannot separate ourselves nowadays. We are all simply living in different rooms of the same house. Each country is a different room. We cannot just close our eyes and say, "It happened to them, it is not my problem." It is already too late for that. When we see that some of the people are doing something wrong in a country, all the other countries should boycott them. If it is clear that they should not be doing certain things, we should all boycott them in every way. We should not go and fight with them, because two wrongs do not make a right.

This is the ancient village method. If a person in the village did something wrong and refused to admit it, do you know what used to happen? The person would not be punished in any way. Instead, everyone would say, "Let us all boycott this rogue. Nobody should even go near this person's house." Of course, nowadays we all have washing machines, dryers, shavers, everything at home. In those days you had to go to the barber to get a shave, send your clothing to a laundryman. Everyone in the village received some service from each of the others. If someone was doing something wrong, immediately there would be a meeting. The leaders, the wise people, would call everyone together and say, "The only way is to boycott him. No barber should go to give him a shave. No laundryman should wash this person's clothes. For good or bad, nobody should go to his place. Ignore him totally." Do you know what used to happen? Within a few days the guilty one would come crying, "I am so sorry for what I did; please, I do not want to be abandoned like this. I realize that I made a mistake."

Ultimately, who is stronger, humanity or God? Certainly God is. So God must be allowing humanity to make these mistakes. It is an indirect way of teaching us lessons. If God thinks that this is the only way we can learn a lesson, He will certainly allow us to continue to make mistakes. He is not ignorant of our suffering. He is watching. He has given us intelligence. He has given us good hearts; and if we are not using them in the right way, then we will have to pay the price for it. If He interferes, He is in a way preventing us from learning that lesson. Suppose the teacher feels sorry that you are struggling and gives you all of the answers to the exercises in the book; you will never learn to solve the problems yourself. Even though you might make mistakes over and over, he or she will still let you keep trying, maybe with a little advice along the way. If you listen well and apply what you are told, you will certainly get the answer. And that is also God's way.

Did you ever look at the end of the almanac where they list all the disasters ever recorded in history? They even say how many lost their lives. We are horrified at the Holocaust, but look at all the millions and millions lost through the so-called natural phenomena. How can that kind-hearted, all-merciful God allow this to happen? If He does not care for us, who does? If He does not take care of us, who will? We cannot even take care of ourselves. Of course He cares for us, but His ways are mysterious. And He will never let us destroy ourselves completely. We may be destroying the beautiful vehicles He gave us, but our true Selves can never be destroyed. So these are all lessons. He let us invent nuclear power, allowed us to use our will to misuse that same power. Now He is making us learn the lesson to use nature's power for the benefit of all and live happily.

How many times would the mother tell her baby, "Don't touch! It's hot!" Still, the baby reaches out again and again until one time it gets burned. Then it has learned its lesson.

That is the same kind of situation we are in now with all the secrets of the universe. Probably when we were living in caves we were happier. Maybe when we got hungry, we might have fought with each other. When one person got a little piece of something, another would have grabbed it from him. But when the hunger was satisfied, they would be playing together again. Look at the animals. Only when they are hungry do they go after food. Even the wild animals are so peaceful; how gently they play. When they are not hungry, they would not even think of attacking another animal. With human beings, even when their stomachs are full they fight and kill. Our basic needs are always taken care of somehow, but that does not seem to be enough for us.

Now we are using our intelligence to probe into various unnecessary things, and we are creating problems that we do not know how to handle. It's like the little fellow who opened the jar that he found on the seashore. He was just walking along the beach when he suddenly saw it. It was nice, shiny, beautiful; but it was sealed. Immediately he got curious and wanted to see what was inside. It was sealed tightly, and he could not open it. There was even a note on the outside, "Please, nobody open this jar!" Of course, after reading that he became even more determined to open it, thinking he would be the first one. He worked hard, pried it open, and as soon as the cork came out, a huge cloud of smoke rose from the jar. He got frightened, and jumped back, looking up at the cloud.

Slowly, slowly, slowly, the cloud took shape and became a huge

21

demon which said, "I am hungry! Thank you for releasing me, but I have to eat now." And he started chasing the boy.

The boy ran and ran, not knowing what else to do. Suddenly he came across a wise man and fell at his feet saying, "Please, please save me, help me."

"What happened?"

"Well, my own curiosity is about to kill me."

By that time the demon was there. "Hey, now I have two people, I will eat both of you."

"All right, if you are hungry," said the wise man. "We are certainly here to feed the hungry. Nobody should go hungry in this world. You can certainly eat us, but please tell us why you are so hungry all of a sudden. At least before you devour us, tell us your story a little so that we can die happily, knowing that we gave our lives for a good cause."

"Oh, is that so? Well, it is really a long story. You know, I was not behaving very well and so I was a menace to many people. One fellow who looked a lot like you, a big guy, he kicked me hard and I went up in a cloud of smoke. Then he put me into the jar and sealed it. I was trapped there for thousands of years; he even threw me into the sea. But luckily the waves carried me to the beach where this fellow released me."

"Ah, don't be foolish. We are not going to believe that. You must be — what — at least one hundred feet tall? And you were inside that little jar?"

"Yes, I am telling you the truth."

"Well, you know, seeing is believing."

"Then I shall prove it to you!" The demon took them both back to the jar, changed into smoke again and went back inside. As soon as he did, of course, the wise man quickly put the cap back on. He told the boy, "Don't you ever go and pry open secrets again, do you understand?"

We need wise men like that today. We do not need wise men to tell us how to handle the powers we have unleashed; that is beyond our capacity. Instead, we need wise men to tell us that we do not need all that, to remind us to be contented. Couldn't we be happy with a little food, a little clothing, a little shelter over our heads? What else do we need? Sun and rain and a little shelter. A little clothing to cover the body. After all, we started with a fig leaf. Modern dress is coming back to that anyway, is it not?

There is plenty to eat if we get hungry. If we get tired, we can sleep. What more do we need? All these things will always be provided, no doubt. Even an ant knows there will be a rainy day. Yet, people spend more than they earn, and then one rainy day they blame others. "Oh, they are not providing enough for us anymore."

It is not only individuals; even corporations act that way. Executives have to have salaries of hundreds of thousands of dollars. There are big expense accounts, big bills for entertainment. And it is called "the cost of doing business." If we live in this kind of greedy way, we certainly will have to learn a lesson in a hard way. It is just egoism, "I did this, I did that first, I have so many of these things." I do not really think that we can blame God for the consequences. He is really teaching us a good lesson, and if we are smart, we will catch on soon.

Power

In my opinion the greatest power is the power to control one's own mind. Learn to control and discipline your own body, senses, desires, thoughts, and ego. You can win the entire world with love, with affection, with service. Look at the great saints, sages, prophets—Buddha, Christ, Mohammed—they were able to win over the whole world. How many billions of people are there following Jesus Christ and Buddha? How were all those hearts won? Not with guns, not with missiles. By love we can win the whole world over to our side. The victory that you win by war, by force, by arms is not the real victory. There is still the seed of vengeance, the seed of enmity left behind. One side says, "We won the war." What happens to the other side? They "lose" the war. Then what will be the relationship between the two parties? The people who lost the war will still be enemies to those who won. The war might have been won, but the people have not been won over. They will go back and wait for an opportunity to bomb the so-called winners. That is why even though one side won the First World War, there was still a World War II.

Rage is a normal reaction to some situations. We cannot expect everyone to be perfectly passive and peaceful; but by exploding, by expressing the rage, one is not going to change the mind of the other person. You might even make the situation worse. By using violence, you might gain a temporary victory, but the other person will still be your enemy. Instead, win the heart of the other person. The real victory is to make your enemy into your friend; then there

25

will be no more wars. Of course, that is a very difficult thing to do. But difficult things must be achieved. Self-control, self-discipline, self-mastery, self-reformation and selflessness; these are the sources of real power that would benefit everybody.

Defense

Naturally we have to defend ourselves against undesirable elements. When I speak against war, I am talking about offensive war. Offense is not good. To defend oneself, however, is a part of Nature. God created the eyes, and He created the lids also to defend the eyes, is it not so? When you feel something coming close to the eyes, you immediately close them. That is an instinctive defense. You have every right to defend yourself. Violence by itself is not bad; it is the motive behind it that makes the difference. With what motive do you go and fight someone? For what reason do you cause violence? Even a doctor inflicts violence on a patient during an operation. No matter how painful that may be, you still pay the doctor; but if somebody on the street cuts you with a knife, you put that person in prison. The knife is the same, the action is the same; it is the motive that is important.

You defend your body; that is the country in which you live. In the same way, you have every liberty to defend your home, your family, your country. But you do not have the liberty to go and cause injury or destroy others for your own gain. When everything else fails in defending yourself, you might even have to kill. But in that you are not meaning to destroy somebody, only to disarm. The Self is indestructible. The Self uses the body. It should use the body for the benefit of everyone; but if the body is misused, if the body itself becomes a weapon to hurt you, you might have to try to stop it. If everything else fails, you might even have to destroy it.

Imagine this situation: An insane person takes a machine gun and begins shooting people who are innocently walking down the street. You are there and have the ability to stop him. What would you do? Would you say, "I don't believe in any kind of violence so I'll just go on my way."? No. You would do whatever you could to end the slaughter. Certainly if you could disarm the gun wielder without killing him, you would do that. But if necessary you would even kill him in order to save others. Sometimes there is no alternative; you must defend others or even yourself.

War can be justified if it is purely for the protection of one's own country. That is the soldier's job, to defend the country. The purpose of war should be to correct injustices. That might cause some pain. It is violent, is it not? But if you have the proper motive, you will not want to hurt anyone or anything unnecessarily. That is the duty of the soldier.

POLITICS

Politics

One of the big political problems now is what to do about terrorism. We should not give in to the demands of terrorists. Once we succumb to a demand, there will be many more such demands all over. That is why these kidnappers and hijackers always seem to win. They get what they want. The only way to stop a hijacker is to refuse to succumb to any demand. They must be shown that they will not get anything that way. No one should give in to them; and if people die as a result, those people will be heroes who died for a noble cause. Aren't we willing to die for a just cause on the battlefield? This too is a battlefield. Principle is more important than life. And principle should be the basis of politics.

We should also take care that we choose sane people as our leaders. Do not elect somebody because she is a relative, or because he is a great orator. Look at the person's character. Is he a noble person? Is she a neutral person? Even the party system creates problems in a way. Individuals should be selected as individuals, that is all. The question should not be, "To which party do you belong?" It should be, "Are you doing this for the sake of the country? Is it beneficial to all the people, including the other party?" All of our representatives should be unbiased, saintly people.

It is not easy to run a country. If a righteous person is asked to serve in this way, he or she will certainly do it. But such a person will never go and push for it. Others should go and beg for that service: "We need you. You are a noble person. You are an upright person. You have neutral vision. We know that you will do something good for our country. We beg you to come and take this position." The way it is now, the candidates go and beg the voters to vote for them. Should I come and beg you to elect me to serve you? If I am serving you, you are the one who is benefited, is it not so? You should come and ask me, request my service. I should not come and try to persuade you to accept my service. That is a common mistake.

If you want to be a candidate, why not simply announce it: "I would like to serve the country in such-and-such position. These are my qualifications and this is what I have done so far as a private citizen." Give a sort of resume to the country. Make your life an open book; state it simply. "This is it. If you like me, elect me." Then just go back home and sleep comfortably. You should not have to run door-to-door for candidacy. Just offer what you have, and if the people do not choose you, it seems they really want the other person for some reason. Even if they make a mistake in that, it does not matter. They will certainly learn a lesson from their mistake. Probably that is the only way God could teach them. It will be His headache, not yours. You just do your job, and leave the rest up to Him.

We should have a policy that no candidate should get any contribution from any citizen or any corporation. The candidates should not even use their own money because each one will have different amounts available. Let the government provide a certain amount of the taxpayers' money so that each qualified candidate may be heard. Each one can have an equal amount of television and radio time, an equal amount for brochures, and so on. In this way, no representative will be obliged to anybody because of financial backing.

Still, the representative may feel obligated to his or her party. Once a person is elected, he should forget about parties and serve the whole country. "No matter what party you belong to, I am your President. I will serve all the people equally." We need those who sit at the top to have equal vision. Once they are elected, they should ignore all the differences. They should not even label themselves as Republican or Democrat, conservative or liberal. If they cannot expand their consciousness beyond their own country, at least within that country they should be neutral to everybody.

The right intention is very important. We should always serve with a clean heart. And once we commit ourselves to doing the job, we should fulfill our promise, no matter what the cost.

When Pandit Nehru became the Prime Minister of India, the first thing he did was to renounce all of his wealth. He gave everything he had to the Congress Party. His feeling was, "I do not want to keep any money for myself. I want to have a clean hand." His follower, Sastri, was even greater. He even sent the money he received as salary to the Friends of India Society. When he died suddenly in a plane crash, there was not even a cent in his home. He did not even have a house of his own. When the government came forward to educate his children, his wife said, "No. As long as he lived he never accepted government money. He simply accepted food and shelter in a government house while he worked as a servant of the people. He never took anything for his personal use, for his family or for me. So it is not right for me to accept anything now either. I will work hard and earn the money to educate my children. The government should not be spending on them. They should not be treated differently than any of the other children in India." That is the kind of saintly, selfless people we need in government today.

Be careful in selecting future candidates. If your leaders are not listening to you, it is not their mistake. It is your mistake; you elected the wrong people. Let us choose the right leadership, starting from the top. And let us demonstrate that we want peace—not just by marching in front of government buildings, but by leading peaceful, loving lives; not only in our own backyard, but around the globe.

Communism and Capitalism

Whenever I meet communists, they ask me, "What do you think about communism?" I tell them, "In its pure form it is a wonderful idea; but you know, I am a better communist than you because spiritual people, or people who follow a religion, are supposed to be the greatest communists." It is true. No religious person can be otherwise. That person may be very dedicated to a system of government that is not communist; it is not government I am talking about here. What is the basic ideal of communism? Live for the sake of everyone, do not live for your personal sake, share everything with everybody. That is real communism. Do not grab everything for yourself. Religion says the same thing, and even goes a step further; that is why I say that it is the greatest communism. Religion says that you should not just share, but you should give away all the excess from what you have. Give away as much as you can. Treat nothing as yours. It all belongs to God. Use what you really need and give the rest. Couldn't this be called communism?

There is no violence in it, no law, no force; just by changing the attitude in the mind, you become a giving person. All the religions teach this. That kind of giving is the real religion. That is why the *Bhagavad Gita* says, even if you cook for the sake of yourself, you are a thief. You should cook for somebody else, first feed others, and then if there is something left over, you may eat it. Naturally there will be something left if you are entitled to it. Do not do anything for yourself, do not worry about your share; just act for the sake of others. That is why I say, do not even think that you are living for your own sake; in fact, we cannot live for ourselves, we are made to live for the sake of others. There is a purpose in our living, which the Cosmic Plan knows; that is why the Cosmic Force wants us to live, and that is why we are living.

Is there anyone who can say that he is living by his own capacity? I do not think so. As we all know, to be alive means we must breathe. The breath is the very life, and you all know that the breath flows in and out. As the breath goes out, we are dying; but each time the air comes back in again. Why? Of course the anatomy books may say it is the involuntary muscles that expand the chest, expand the lungs, and the air is drawn in. Still, they say "involuntary"—it is not voluntary, it is not your conscious act but something unconscious, something beyond your control. Then who is controlling it? The Cosmic Will. The Cosmic Will wants you to live, so every time the air goes out, it sends the air back in. Somebody is taking care of it. When I say "somebody," I am not speaking about an entity sitting somewhere on a big throne; I mean the Cosmic Will, the Higher Plan, of which we are all a part. It is very difficult for the part to know the whole, whereas the whole knows each and every part. That is why the whole wants the part to do its work, and so takes care of it. When the work is over, even though we want to live, the breath does not come back in; it goes out once and for all. We may not want to die, but we still die. It is not in our hands. When your part in the Cosmic Plan is over for the time being, you are taken away from this body.

So everything is controlled by the Cosmic Will. When such is the case, why should we grab things for ourselves? That is why the real religious life is in living for the sake of others. Even at the altar, we give up everything in the name of the Lord: "Oh Lord, everything is Yours. I am Thine, all is Thine, Thy will be done." Don't we say that? Is that not a sort of communism? Instead of being forced to give things up, you yourself come forward and say, "Here it is, I surrender everything to You. I dedicate everything to the universe, to others. Even my very life. . .let me not live for my sake, let me not act for my sake—but for the sake of all."

Do not immediately label me as a communist now. I believe in all the "isms." Basically, all are needed. We need capitalism, we need imperialism, we need communism. You are not the same always in your own life. Sometimes you act like a capitalist; at other times you act like a communist. Probably when you go home, you are imperial royalty to your children. When you go to the club you are a communist, a comrade. When you go to your office you are a kind of servant. We all have many different roles in life.

Ultimately, what should we do? We should feel the oneness of humanity. Not everyone can be a capitalist. Who is a capitalist? The one who puts up more money. Money never stays with everyone equally. That is why I do not approve of trying to use force or law to ensure material equality. It can never happen.

Maybe today we could say, "Everybody, bring all your money here. Nobody should keep even one cent. If you have a penny, bring it. If you have a hundred dollars, bring it. Bring all the money and we will divide it all equally." For how long could you keep it that way? In two days, you would see one person developing that ten dollars into a hundred dollars. You would see another person spending the whole ten dollars and going and begging for another five. You are only dividing the money, not the intelligence. You cannot bring all the brains together and divide them equally. You can never make people think the same way. As long as there are differences in thinking, ways and means will vary. The one who loses money will lose; the one who accumulates will accumulate. And the one who accumulates money will put it back into some business and make even more. There is nothing wrong with that. Because of someone's interest in making more money, he or she gives you the opportunity to work. Such a person creates jobs.

We are always complaining about unemployment. When someone builds a big factory, a hundred thousand more people can work. Take the Alaska Pipeline for example. How many people are going to get jobs from that? Who will put up the money for the Alaska Pipeline? A capitalist. If it were not for the capitalists, you might not even have a job. Not that I am praising the capitalists. Without those workers, the capitalists could not make a cent. There is a relationship between them, a mutual help. One should never hate the other. It is not the capitalist's mistake, having that much money. Is it the mistake of a big millionaire to be born into a millionaire's house? He or she happened to be born there; why didn't you do that? You could have been born there. You went and took birth in an ordinary home. You have to go out and work for even ten dollars a day. Whose mistake is that?

We should not curse people or criticize people; instead, everyone should understand these principles. Those who have should share with the have-nots. The people who have little should not hold a grudge against the people who have a lot. Even if some of the "haves" do not give, that is their *karma*, their destiny.

What I am saying is this: Do not have any negative feeling toward the people who have money, and do not try to take it by force. It is theirs. If they give, fine. If they do not give they may lose it one day, one way or another, because it is not good to accumulate money and not use it. They are going to learn a lesson; but until they get the lesson, you are not going to be able to enlighten them. Just accept it and do what you can. These seeming differences will always be there in life. You see this in your own body. We have five fingers on each hand. Not all of them are equal, but which of them is inferior and which superior? When we do some work, all the fingers come together.

In this kind of understanding is where the real communism lies. That means, in the name of universal brotherhood we all love each other and live as one. Give and take, care and share. You teach people to care and share by changing the heart—not by force. Nothing can be done by force. Law can never instill ideas into your head. In fact, there was a follower of Mahatma Gandhi named Vinoba Bhave—you might have heard of him—who talked to the rich people, converted their minds and convinced them to give much of their land and money to the poor people. The law could not do that. He got thousands of acres from the landowners and distributed five acres to each person. If the same thing had been done in the name of the law, the people would have resisted.

Real equality can come only by opening hearts, never by force, never by violence. And that equality is the ultimate motive behind all of these social principles—socialism or communism or capitalism—one way or another. There must be different roles. The head or the brain is the capital, it just sits there. The hand does everything, but the head directs it. The hand should not say, "Hey, why do you sit there and direct me? Why shouldn't you also come and do this? If I am in the mud picking up rocks, you should be too." The head should not feel that the hand is in any way inferior; the head can sit and think and think, but without the hand, none of its brilliant plans would be achieved. There is no superiority or inferiority. Everything was made for its own purpose. With that understanding, we can all work together to achieve all of our goals in life.

The West

When a nice lunch is prepared and served, who will be the first one at the table? The one who is the hungriest. The others will come slowly, talking, sitting in front of the plate and appreciating the way everything is prepared. When you are not that hungry, you are not so eager to eat. In the same way, religious ideas, spiritual ideas, are appreciated and followed by people who are hungry for them. The West is hungry for this now. Spiritual hunger means you want spirituality and that comes first; all the rest comes afterward. So the people in the West have achieved everything materially, and they are tired of it. They have not found any peace or comfort or happiness in it. Even with all the material, scientific and technological growth, all the conveniences, time-savers and luxuries, they still feel something lacking.

When you get really tired of the world, you think of God. In the Bible, when people wanted to follow Lord Jesus, he told them, "Come, renounce everything, take up the cross and follow me." Many in the West are renouncing the world in a way. It is not something forced, but a decision that people have come to on their own. In the East people are told, "Renounce the world, it is not going to give you permanent peace and joy." They hear the words, but they do not understand the message. The West has understood this from experience. You can see this very clearly in the U.S.; many young people who came from rich parents with plenty of money, nice homes, nice cars, radios, televisions, all kinds of comforts, just walked away from it. Why? They were tired of all that; they did not seem to find any peace and comfort in it.

Why are there problems in the West? The reason is the same one for problems all over the world. It is mainly due to the wrong attitude of the human mind. People today seem to have lost the proper approach to things. They all seem to be filled with selfishness, greed. We cannot blame the material things themselves. If, in the name of ecology, we shut down the electric generating stations, we would not be able reach so many people through microphones, printing presses, recordings. So much good can be done through electricity; we do need it.

The question is, how do we use it? How much do we use and for what purpose? It is the attitude of the mind that is to be changed, not the material things outside. There is nothing wrong with all these inventions. We should know how to use them, and we should use them in a way that is totally free from selfishness. As it is now, all these technological inventions are mostly used for the destruction of humanity. But they could just as well be used for constructive purposes.

Then what makes someone use them for destruction? It is greed, pride, ego. Take for example, the aerospace industry. We have so many jumbo jets, but I hear that at least half of them are empty. At the same time, they want a larger plane now. Why? Because somebody else has produced a larger one. It is just for the sake of competition, human pride. If we used these things just to fulfill our need—not our greed—then this ecology problem would not arise. We seem to always feel we must compete. For the sake of competition we just do more and more and more without even knowing why. Fortunately we are beginning to understand this. Especially the present generation; they understand this well. That is why they do not want these things anymore. They do not have this false pride inside. Maybe the older people would want the prestige of an SST. But the younger generation is saying, "We are happy without an SST. We don't need it. We don't want it." There is a kind of contentment in them. They realize the shallowness of these things.

That is why I feel that the West is not really collapsing. It is on its way up again. I have very good hope that through the younger generations we are going to see a peaceful society one day soon, and a useful society too. With all the resources in the hands of the new generation, certainly the whole world is going to be benefited. Each country has so much to give. We really waste a lot. The amount we waste in one day in the U.S. alone is enough to take care of a poor country for at least a month. Just one day's wastage. In every way: food, clothing, electricity. We say there is an energy crisis, yet how many bulbs are burning needlessly? During the daytime you see rows and rows of lights burning in all the buildings. What does that mean? It is just adding to the crisis.

People gather things without even thinking of whether they really need them or not. Once they have gathered the things, they worry about how to keep them, how to maintain them. Then they are caught. When you get really stuck, then you realize, "I have gathered too much. I don't want all this anymore." If you are not going to get the point simply by using your intelligence, then the very things you gather will teach you the lesson. That is the purpose of nature. It is constantly teaching us lessons.

Is not pollution a great teacher? It is telling us, "You have done a lot of damage through your greed. You can survive, you can live happily without so many things. Your grandparents lived much more happily than you with your so-called advancement. You are not happy. Why don't you go back to that state?" We learn that way, by our mistakes. One person can also learn from the mistakes of another; each one does not have to make all of the mistakes.

Right now we are learning from the mistakes of our parents and grandparents. We are seeing that nobody seems to be content. And that is making us wonder where happiness comes from. We have more things than ever before in history, but nobody seems to be fulfilled by all these things. A multi-millionaire wants one more million. The one who rules a big country wants to rule a part of the next country also. Where is the end to it all? When are we going to be happy?

Ultimately we are forced to look within, and when we do, we find out that real happiness is there itself, inside. Our very nature is happiness. Somehow we keep on forgetting that, and so we look for it outside. That is ignorance. We think that the things outside are bringing us happiness. Unfortunately, they seem to be bringing a little happiness followed by a lot of unhappiness. Eventually we learn, "I can be happy without any of these things." Then some people go to the other extreme; they leave a palatial house and go live in a teepee. The teepee does not bring them happiness either. At least while sitting in the teepee they will realize that contentment comes from within. They will walk with all happiness and bring happiness to others.

Happiness is another form of peace. A peaceful person is a happy person. Why do all these peace talks fail? Because those who are talking do not have peace in themselves. They sit around the table talking about peace, but within their minds each one wants to grab a little more for his side. It is a kind of business. Once we realize the peace and the happiness within, we will bring that peace with us everywhere we go. Once we start to bring peace to the conference table, we are paving the way for the whole world to find peace and joy.

Our recent history has shown us this. Our material comforts are bringing more and more calamities. God alone can save us now. Realizing the spirit and loving everybody as your own spirit is the only way to find peace and joy. That seems to be the revelation on this planet today, and that idea is growing all over. Imagine ten or fifteen years ago, would you even have been sitting reading this book? You would have been somewhere exciting, going out, having parties. Yes. Imagine, sitting like this and reading a book about achieving world peace by being selfless. Don't you agree with me? Just ten years ago, what would you have thought of all this? But today people are becoming more and more determined to find peace. That is why I have a big hope for the future. You are all going to make this world a beautiful heaven, no doubt.

America

America is leading the whole world in many ways, but they are all in the material field. The time has come for America to help the whole world with spirituality also. The country itself is becoming a whole. That is why all across the length and breadth of the United States, we see thousands and thousands of people who are spiritually-minded. Let all of our actions and all our arts express our common spirit and our universal brotherhood.

Often we hear groups of people shouting that we should "fight for peace." I still do not understand how they are going to find peace if they are fighting. Before attempting to achieve anything else, let us first find peace within ourselves. The future of the whole world is in our hands. The entire world is watching; the entire world is going to know what the American people can do for humanity. So every one of us should feel responsible for the whole world. Certainly we are all seeing a new awakening. I always speak with pride about the present American generation, the modern youth, because there is a lot of awakening in them. You do not even see it this much in other countries. Take for example in Buckingham, Virginia, in the ashram where I am staying. There are almost one hundred people. They all feel that it is their home. It is not mine or yours. It is ours. Whatever they get they share. It is one big family. We call it Yogaville.

My dream is that one day the entire country will live that way. With everyone sharing. Then the country itself could also share with all the other countries. The whole world could be like Yogaville. We know that there are enough resources for all of us. Nobody needs to starve, nobody needs to suffer on this earth. We have plenty, plenty, plenty. But we do not care and we do not share. If all of a sudden we grow another thousand tons of potatoes, we are willing to dump them into the ocean just to keep the price up. How many times has this happened? Instead, if we grow an extra amount of something, why not give it away? Probably somebody else has a surplus of something else. Bring it here. Exchange things instead of constantly converting everything into dollars.

If only you could see in front of you all the food that is wasted in America in one day alone, the food that just gets thrown out. You cannot begin to imagine how much we waste. Many people do not even know how much to cook for one meal. So much of the food that is served in restaurants never gets eaten. At the same time, we know that others are starving. Excuse me for saying this. I get a little vehement about these things sometimes because I feel so sad about it. The whole world can be happy only if we learn how to stop wasting and how to start sharing.

Our national advancement or profit should not be at the cost of somebody else. On the other hand, we should do the best we can within our country. If we produce more than we need, we should even share with others. Unfortunately even sharing sometimes seems to be big business. It is called "aid", but it is actually a bribe. The minute the receivers stop listening to the helping country and quit doing what is expected, the aid is stopped. We should be more open. We should think of the people and feel, "Because we can afford to, we are aiding them. We are helping them. We have plenty, so of course we should give." No country should give and make demands in return.

In fact, the whole world should be like that. Even the poorest country has something to give. That is why sometimes people even talk about having a world government. In the U.S., for example, we have different states, but they are united. Likewise, why not have different nations, united. The U.N. itself could form a United Nations government, a federal government for the whole world. Resources in a richer area could be passed on to where there is a need. You could just take what you need for yourself, and the surplus could be given for others' use. If they have oil and you need oil, get some oil from them. If you have more than enough food, give some food. If they have some technology, get technology. Like that, we could have an exchange of things and ideas. That would be a beautiful way to live, with the whole world acting as one family. We should not ignore the rest of the world, nor should we offer them "help" for our own benefit alone. We should always think of the whole, and if we can afford to help others, we should give our help freely.

We should be thinking about all these things, about the way in which we live. Every year we spend millions and billions of dollars in so many harmful ways. Why do we do it? To make money, that is all. Is this the way to become rich? By selling poison to others? Even after the Surgeon General says that smoking is not good, billboards go up — thousands of dollars for one billboard. "Come on. It naturally refreshes you." Imagine the amount of money that is going up in smoke. At the same time, you are asked to give money to cure cancer. For which cause is more money spent? Thousands are spent in curing cancer. Millions are spent in producing cancer.

I tell this to the present youth. At least you should come forward and stop all these things. If we really want a healthy world tomorrow, we cannot just be happy ourselves while our neighbors are unhappy. If you are happy, do something to make others happy too. We have to be more responsible. We have to do the right thing. We have to care and share.

Fortunately, we can see that happening more and more now. I am very proud of it. Coast to coast, all over the country I see it. Everywhere people are spiritually-minded, acting on the principle of universal brotherhood. Unfortunately all these nice things are rarely reported. That is not considered to be worth printing. If somebody gets married, it appears in small print. If somebody gets divorced, it is in the headlines. The news media also should change their attitude and present the beautiful events too. Many, many nice things are happening. I tell the media people, "Please, you are the makers of the world. Present the right things. The nonsense will always be there. Every house has a toilet. Why don't you look at the beautiful living room? Instead, you go into the toilet. It's not so nice, but that is what you want to present. As if you didn't have a toilet in your own house."

The bad things are there. There is no need to publicize them all constantly. Many problems are made worse because we emphasize them. We should even ignore some of these things. Take for example the assassinations. It is true, some of the presidents were assassinated. Okay, the assassin was a crazy fellow; he murdered a world leader. Of course we all want to know what happened, but do we need to know the killer's entire history? Who his father was, who his grandfather was, where he studied? Overnight he becomes a historical figure. We do not even know that much about Jesus, but we have to know all about the man who shot the President because he wanted to impress a movie star. They spend pages and pages and pages, for weeks and weeks, writing all about him, showing pictures of him. Naturally, somebody says, "Hey, if I assassinate a famous person, overnight I can also become famous." This kind of publicity induces others to do the same thing.

Making such people famous is the wrong psychology. I am bringing all this up because the present generation can do so much in this area. The future is in your hands. We older people are all on the verge of saying goodbye; you are tomorrow's citizens. We have made some terrible mistakes. At least learn from our mistakes and do not repeat them. Make the world a better place. Make it one worth living in.

That is why it is so important to choose our leaders carefully. In many cases we cannot even trust them anymore. Still you cannot blame them. It is a democratic country, so who made the leaders? You did. Your vote put them there. Why did you vote? "Oh, because I was fascinated by his talk." Yes. You gave millions of dollars. Maybe not you and I, but many of the people who voted would have given money for that purpose: "Yes, if I put him there, he will do everything for my sake. Whatever I want he will pass. He won't pass any bill against me."

We call our country a democracy, but it is not truly a democracy unless our elected representatives represent all of the people. We have to carefully consider and cast our vote for the right person. It is not that I say we will never make a mistake, or that a mistake cannot be corrected. If, after a while, the majority finds out that a leader is not doing the job well, they should be able to throw that person out of office. The candidates get elected by making big promises. Once they get in, if you see that they are not the right people and are not doing their jobs, why should you keep them? If one of them was your employee, wouldn't you fire that one then and there? Would you wait for two years, four years, six years? Ultimately it is in our hands. "Of the people, by the people, for the people." We should have the right to make a mistake, and the authority to correct it. But we do not have the right to condemn other people, as if we are totally blameless ourselves. And we should not constantly publicize the undesirable things so much; let it be over and done with.

You are part of the whole show. Each one has contributed consciously or unconsciously at least a little to this situation. Open your eyes. Do something to change it. We cannot just continue like this, making the same mistakes over and over, again and again. It is time for us to love the whole universe, to see the whole world as our home. Be neutral to everyone. Do not ever discriminate against anybody for any reason. See the spirit, the soul of everybody, and not just a piece of skin or a pound of flesh. The body is nothing but a bundle of flesh and bones. The mind is nothing but a tape recorder.

Our modern life has become so complicated in all aspects. Let us be simple like children. I would never deny the capacity of our intelligence, but we should not give too much prominence to that. The heart should come first, and the intellect should come after. Let your innocence, your pure heart, lead your life. The intelligence can follow.

It is high time for us to realize this. In every field, as a whole nation. We are still feeling the excitement and the pride of sending the space shuttle up and back. Is it not so? Nobody had ever done that before. We spent billions of dollars for that. What a great achievement. It went up, went around the globe thirty-six times,

49

came down at the appointed hour, landed at the exact spot. That is a wonderful achievement, it is true. There can be no doubt about it.

If we can achieve such a great thing in space, shouldn't we be able to achieve something equally great right on the surface of the earth? Why can't we be proud of saying, "Look at our country. Everybody is safe. There is no theft in this country. There is no crime in this country. All the judges are unemployed. All the lawyers are looking for some other job because there are no court cases. All the police officers are sitting and sleeping. Nobody is violating any law anywhere. No door has locks." Go to New York and look at the doors. From top to bottom, there are rows of locks. Ten locks with bars behind. At the same time, you have gone around the world thirty-six times and have come back. We are proud of that; but can we be proud of these domestic problems? Do we want to do anything about these things? It seems that we want to go around the globe, around the cosmos, instead. Which is more urgent? The Space Program is a good thing. But our nation seems to be taking pride in this kind of superficial prestige, while there is so much that needs to be done for the people of the country.

Don't think people are starving only in Ethiopia while America is rich. There are people in this country sleeping outside with cardboard boxes for houses. And even with all that we still say, "Oh, America is a rich country, land of opportunity." You go all the way to India or Africa, take a picture of a little child who is all skin and bones and then come back and say, "Help!" What about your next door neighbor here? We do not want these nasty things to be known to the outside world, but it is still there.

We should help people everywhere, even right in our own backyard. It is a known fact that every given hour the entire world spends a billion dollars for arms. Every hour a billion dollars is being spent somewhere. All that money could be used to improve the life of people. Wouldn't the whole world be much happier that way?

We always blame others, but if we brought about a change in ourselves first, we would not have to be afraid of anybody. There is a proverb in India that says, "A cobra always hides in a small hole." Do you know the reason? Because it has poison. The other snakes just simply roam around everywhere; they never have to hide because they do not have poison. What a beautiful example for us to learn from. The poisonless snakes simply roam around freely and fearlessly. Even when they see you they do not run quickly. A cobra would never do that. It will run and hide at the least noise or movement. In the same way, the venomous people always take shelter. Because they are venomous, they are afraid of others; they think everybody will hurt them. If you are a clean-hearted, harmless person, you don't have to be worried about anybody.

If a person seems to be a little undesirable in some way, you can make the person desirable by your proper attitude. Then he or she becomes your friend. But if you constantly call someone enemy, enemy, enemy, you can be sure one day that person will be your enemy. Actually that is the problem America now faces with the Soviet Union. Every minute these two countries talk about each other as deadly enemies. At the same time, each one invites the other to come sit and talk. I don't understand this kind of friendliness. You curse them behind their backs; you have nothing good to say about them. Do you think they don't know that? I would not call these "friendly talks" friendly at all. Each side is looking for opportunities to better its own position. The "talk" is not coming from the heart. They are also on guard; can you blame them? These people insisting they talk seem to be cunning; they say they want to be friends, but at the same time they are acting like enemies. Is it any wonder they feel they have to be prepared? This kind of mistrust creates more and more problems. It is really a pity.

In a very real sense, no military action can ever bring lasting peace. Violence stems from violence; it can never eradicate violence. We have every right, freedom and duty to help others for their welfare and their betterment. Send them food, clothing, building materials, but not arms and ammunition. That is not the right thing. We have done that many times, and we have not achieved anything great by that. Yet we continue. Tell me one country that has received our military help and found peace. I am not talking about an innocent country under attack. (In the case of someone innocent being attacked, we should always help defend them.) I am talking about greed—selling arms and ammunition for money. If we sincerely want to help, we can help in other ways—with food, education, the needs of daily life. But we should not interfere in their internal fighting and call it "aid." Suppose tomorrow you have some problems here. What if some other country came and gave "aid" to one section? Would you be happy?

It goes even further than that. The biggest war nowadays is the war of ideology. Constantly we talk about "communism, communism, communism," as if it were something terrible. What about this "ism?" Is it all simply flowing milk and honey here? Can everyone walk freely on the road, any time of the day or night? I am not saying they are perfect either. They also make mistakes, but what right do we have to criticize them when we have our own problems? Don't we read in the Bible, "Take care of the beam in your own eye before you look at the speck in another's eye?"

We constantly talk about communism. As if communism is going to kill the whole world and we are all here to save the whole world. That attitude in itself is creating more enmity. We even have mock fights as if the Soviets are on their way. We are constantly, day and night, thinking of the Soviet Union as our enemy. From the Pentagon to the pulpit we are condemning that country, treating the people as total enemies. Why can't we respect their ideology? "That's your way, all right, go ahead. If yours is right, the whole world will know. Set your example. If it works, the whole world will see and want to follow." It is the same for all the "isms." Set an example; let those who like follow. Neither communism nor capitalism should be forced upon people.

We need to change our vision so that we can change our future. In fact, I would even go so far as to say we should take more responsibility for solving these problems because we contributed more to them. Who made the atomic bombs, hydrogen bombs, nuclear bombs first in this world? The Americans. The Americans made them, piled them up. They even dropped one and saw how horrible it was. Did we stop there? No. We continued to make bombs hundreds of times more powerful, thousands of times more powerful.

52

Naturally any other country would wonder, "What is this? What are we going to do? We have to protect ourselves." Not only have we made bombs, but we have forced the other countries to make bombs too. So we are the cause. Now people say, "They have more than we do, so we should have still more." Because the Americans started the whole thing, we should start the other way also. We should apologize for that and say, "Sorry, we are the cause for all these problems. Here, we are going to stop doing this, please follow us, trust us." It is the fear and mistrust that are causing all the problems. Human greed is killing us.

The only thing we, as citizens, can do is raise our voices, but not in a violent way. Peacefully show your opposition to your leaders, and at the same time do not depend on your own strength. There is a power even higher than the nuclear power. We should try to get help from that higher source; we should pray. When we pray, our prayers should be for the peace and the welfare of all, not just for "our side." God created the other side too. Do you think He is going to listen to us and destroy them on our behalf? I don't think so. If they have made some mistakes, He will see to it that they learn from those mistakes in His own time and in His own way. If we also make the same mistakes in trying to stop them, know that He will take care to see that we also learn from our mistakes.

We seem to be trusting a lot in physical force, technical force, material force. I even jokingly tell people, "You don't want to believe in God. You don't even want to teach your children about God in the classroom, but you believe in the dollar. Ask your own dollar what it believes in. The dollars all say, 'We trust in God.' The dollar trusts in God, you trust in the dollar; therefore you trust in God only through the dollar." It is not only the Americans. In so many places money has taken on the greatest importance. We have come to that level. We are simply losing our souls by that kind of thinking. We don't seem to even remember that there is a creator, there is a God—an Almighty One—who will take care of everything. He took care of all our needs before the dollar was invented, and He will continue to take care of us even when the dollar fails.

Recently, one of the Senators came to the Ashram to visit the clinic. He came because of his own health problems, but he was so impressed with what he saw here that he wanted me to come to a luncheon at the Capitol. He had invited a few other Senators and members of Congress, and we all had lunch together. There they were asking, "We are all talking about the nuclear freeze and related topics. Is there anything that can be done? What is your feeling about it? Tell us, please."

When people ask, I tell them what I feel. I said, "It is not a job for us. We have made a big mess of the whole thing. Man cannot undo it anymore. You people have to set aside a little time, even in your Senate, in your meetings—at least a minute or two before each session—for silent meditation and prayer. All of you pray. Even a nuclear freeze is not going to help. We need sincere prayer and honest negotiation; not cunning, diplomatic talks. And stop talking about your enemies. . .constantly calling them 'enemy,' having mock fights as if they were dropping bombs on you. If you are so afraid of them, how will you ever be able to start trusting them? If you do not trust them, what is the idea of trying to fool everyone by shaking hands in space? You may be shaking hands up there, but at the same time you are shaking the whole world here with your bombs. What kind of diplomacy is that? It is time to open the heart and talk from the heart, not from the head.

"If you want to negotiate, some of you people who believe in this heart-to-heart talking should go and meet with them as friends, not as enemies. I believe in complete trust in the other fellow, and open discussion. Even more than these two, I believe in sincere prayer. Begin every session with prayer. All of you should believe in prayer. Do you think of God only when you come into office and put your hand on the Bible and say, 'I do'?

"What kind of diplomacy is this? You put your hand on the Bible and take an oath for an important office, but you do not allow your children to read that Bible in school. The fact that you take an oath on a holy scripture means you believe in God. Don't you want the future generation to believe in God also? Then let them read the Bible along with the other scriptures of all the world's religions. How can it hurt them? They can be taught that no scripture is superior or inferior; all should be respected while the child continues to practice his or her own path. If you read all the scriptures, you would see that they are all saying the same thing: do not kill each other."

They all said, "Yes, you are right. We really don't have an open heart in this situation. We don't trust people. Our negotiations are made on mistrust, not on trust." I said, "That is why the negotiations fail."

Sincere prayer and peaceful demonstration is the way. There is no other hope for us.

OUR WORLD

World

Who creates war? The bombs do not drop by themselves. It is the people behind them, the human minds that create war. If we want peace, where should we begin? With the minds of the people. If the minds are changed, the world will be changed. There is a saying, "As the man, so the world; as the mind, so the man." Change the mind, you change the person; and change the person, you change the community or the society or the nation or the world. Yoga is one beautiful method by which we can change our minds. It educates us to live a selfless life, to lead a dedicated life. Yoga simply means coming together. That is real communion. If you cannot have communion with your own neighbor, how are you going to have communion with God? Your neighbor is God in a visible form. Yet, you want to have communion with an invisible God sitting somewhere up in heaven. First let us have communion with our own plants, our own pets, our own babies, our own neighbors— next door and around the globe. We need to use spiritual teachings like Yoga to help us have real love for one another.

Even war is based on love, but that love is misplaced or limited in some way. If you want to throw a bomb on another country, you may feel that you're doing it for the sake of your country, because you love your country. All right, you love your country, but don't you think the other person will love his or her own country in the same way? Why don't you expand this love for your nation into a love for the whole world? If your love is universal, how can you bomb someone else? Those people are your brothers and sisters.

The whole world is like a body. If not treated, an infection in one part will spread throughout the whole body. Every part will be affected. Likewise, if we want to be happy, we should work for the happiness of all people everywhere. That is the only way to achieve real peace and contentment. We like to think that we are free, but are we really free in fact? No. We are all bound to each other; and at the same time, we are all afraid of each other. Once we understand that we are all interconnected, we will no longer consider fighting as a solution to our problems. Instead, we will want to reach out to each other. We will want to be friends. It would be a greater freedom to stop hiding behind our arms and bravely stretch out a hand.

Unless the human mind is freed from greed, jealousy and hatred, there will be more and more wars. If you free your own mind of all these problems, at least that little part of the world will be free from trouble. If we want a peaceful world outside, let us begin with ourselves. If we want peace outside, we must have it within first. If we want a world free from violence, we should free ourselves from every kind of violence. That is where Yoga has a message not only for individuals, but for the entire world.

I consider this a transitory period. We are witnessing a great change. When a seedling is transplanted, at first its leaves wither and fall. It has to face that stage; that is part of the process of getting rooted in the earth. It cannot live in the nursery always. In the same way, I see a very bright future for humankind; we are slowly getting rooted. This itself is the proof of what is to come.

I really feel we are going to see a better world. In fact, we are see-ing it already. I am a person who travels constantly around the globe. Wherever I go, I see a marked difference between the generations. Many of the older people are learning good lessons from the younger ones. Even in the United States, many, many parents are opening up to the real natural beauty of what spiritual life is because of their children. With this modern generation, I do not think there will be any more war. It is the political leaders who are creating all the wars. The ordinary people just want to be peaceful. We have seen that in the Middle East—Arab and Israeli soldiers hugging and kissing each other when they parted. The rivalry is only at the topmost level.

Among religions this is also true. The common people do not worry about what religion you belong to. They feel we are all brothers and sisters. The real rivalry is among religious leaders. Many of them label people: "That one is a demon worshiper. She is this. He is that."

The Education Minister in Sri Lanka once asked me, "Swami, is there any way of avoiding all these religious and political fights among the people?"

I said, "Yes, I have a way. But to make it possible you must make me the dictator of the country."

"What?"

"Yes, because too many heads will always create trouble. That is why God kept one head on two shoulders. When one head becomes two, see how complicated it becomes. There can only be one head for one body. Likewise there should be one head for one country. Too many heads always fight, compete, run for elections. They never sit. They literally run, is it not so? So, you would have to make me the dictator for just three days, not more than that."

"Well, I do not really have the power to make you the dictator, but at least tell me what you would do."

"Okay, I will tell you. I would immediately charter two big ships. I would put all the political heads on one ship, and all the religious heads on another ship. Then I would send them to a deserted island. As soon as the ships leave the port there will be harmony, and the people will simply embrace each other. They will all feel like one family. Each leader wants a group of his own, wants to compete with the other leaders. They should realize that this is not the way. They should have the proper understanding among themselves. There are many different ways, and we shouldn't try to change that. We should be aware that the ultimate goal of them all is a common one. There should not be any rivalry. Only when this is achieved will we find peace. Otherwise, it will always be like this."

We should just rise above all the differences and see our spiritual oneness; we should learn to love each other and to always appreciate the nice things that people do. We should not always be pinpointing their mistakes. If we keep on talking about mistakes, then sooner or later we will find ourselves making those same mistakes—"as you think, so you become." If, instead, you keep on talking about the good things, you will become good. You will forget all these superficial differences. The physical and mental differences are just on the surface. We do not need to label or deny people because of them. All the distinctions—village, country, caste, color, community—are just superficial. If you go a little deeper, where is the black and where is the white? Where is the yellow and where is the brown? It is only skin deep. The spirit has no black or white or brown or yellow. This is the real spiritual life: talking in terms of spirit, loving in terms of spirit. That is the real Yoga or unity or communion. We cannot have communion with God without having communion with our own fellow beings.

"My community first, my family first, my country first. . .I am even ready to die for my country." We hear such things over and over. It is good to love your country, no doubt, but you should love the other person's county also. You have a special love for your own mother, but does your loyalty to her mean that you should dislike other mothers?

If we all feel that we belong to the entire world, what is the country next to us? It is more or less our next-door apartment or even the next room in the same house. Because you love your room, would you go and disturb your sister's room in the same house? If we love *only* our own country, it is a kind of limited love, which might also be called selfishness. Not that you should not love yourself, but when you love yourself, you should also love everybody else in the same way. When we do not do that, we see these political wars and other problems coming up. Each country wants to be the topmost, so it tries to keep the others down. Then the fear and the rivalry come in. Why is there an arms race going on now? Because each one is afraid of the other. In a way, the world is not really healthy right now. A person with a lot of fear cannot be healthy however many resources he or she has. The same is true of a country.

If today the United States and the Soviet Union would think of the entire world as theirs and use the resources that go into arms to help the other countries develop and to distribute resources equally, they could be more or less the caretakers or the parents of the entire world. They could be the friends of all, and the entire world would be happy. Instead, they think that they can control others by force, that they can bring peace with an arms race. It is very wrong thinking. Peace can never be brought by war or by force, only by love.

Look at all the great people like Jesus, Buddha, Mohammed. How many millions love them even today and worship them? Why? Because they loved the entire humanity. Unfortunately, even in that people have segregated themselves as followers of Christ, followers of Buddha, et cetera; and they say, "Mine is the best, yours is no good." Then religious wars come in. It is all based on limited, selfish love. Whenever you put limitations on your love, you are separating yourself from others, you are fencing yourself in. We should just open our minds and our hearts. Even just imagining, "I belong to the whole world and the entire world is my family," will make you so happy and peaceful. That is how all our great sages and saints wanted us to be. That is how they became sages and saints. It seems that many people only read the scriptures, and do not follow them in their lives.

The other day some people asked me if there are catastrophes in store for us. The answer I gave was, "Maybe." I think probably they wanted me to give them a day and year, or at least an approximate date. In that case the answer is, "Maybe tomorrow." But we do not need to worry about that. Remember, whatever is created can be destroyed. Don't ever forget that. What was put together will get separated. At a wedding the minister says, "What God has put together, let not man put asunder." God has the authority to do that, but not man. Remember that. God put it together, so it is not your place to take it apart. If at any time it has to be cut, let the One who put it together be the one to take it apart. He will do it one day, no doubt. Anything that has been brought together will be separated

63

one day. If there is a coming, there will be a going. If there is a making, there will be a breaking. They are inseparable. Body comes, body goes; building comes, building goes. Dust to dust, ashes to ashes. Can you tell me one thing that is permanent in this world? No. Don't worry about catastrophes. What do we have to lose? We might lose our old model bodies, but we will get new bodies, so don't worry. Why should we be afraid? Anything that is immortal will never die. Even if there is no earthquake, how long are you going to live in this body? Maybe another fifty years, sixty years, one hundred years, one hundred and twenty years. One day you are going to say goodbye. Why worry about it? A hero dies once. If you have constant fear, you are destroying your whole life. It makes you die every minute; it is a sort of suicide. Let death come to us once, not constantly, every night and every day. Be bold and be brave, and don't worry about all these things. Just know that there is a purpose behind everything, and that the purpose is always for the good of all.

There are certain things that have been revealed to the great seers, and they have spoken about them. Unfortunately, we are trying to interpret what they say. These revelations are to be understood on a different level. It is our minds that interpret. If our minds are already colored, our interpretation also will be colored. Instead of worrying about doomsday, let us just do what the saints and sages asked us to do. Then there is no need to worry about the future. That is the reason much of the future is purposely not revealed to us. If God, or the Cosmic Awareness, thought we would be benefited by knowing the future, it would not be very difficult to leave the door open. We would know. We do not need to go running around to astrologers and palmists to get predictions. What we need to know will be made known to us. God is not that stingy. If it were beneficial, God would tell us right away. Instead God says, "Why worry about tomorrow? Why worry about the past? Past is past. The future is not in your hands. But the golden present is in your hands. Think of the golden present. Do what it is right to do now. Sow what is to be sown now. Certainly you will reap later on." When people worry about reaping, in their worry they forget to sow. What will they reap then? First of all you should not worry, and then you should do something useful.

You might have a beautiful dream, "After ten years I will have many varieties of fruits and flowers in my garden, and I will go and pick them all and give them to everyone. No one will go hungry. The whole world will be beautiful and full." You can sit there, imagining all that, and really enjoy your vision. But you are wasting your time if all you do is think about it. Use that time to go and dig a hole. At least plant one seed. Sow the right seed now, in the golden present, and you will have a golden future.

In a way the questioning generations are all sowing good seeds. They are interested in finding out the truth, in learning about themselves, in becoming better people. Those seeds will bear fruit. With people like this all over the globe, the world will have a wonderful future. Many people say to me, "The world is going to collapse at any moment." I do not think so. I have confidence in the people who are sowing the seeds of health and happiness, of peace and goodness. This world is going to be filled with better people, people who love each other, care for each other. It is already happening, and all of you are the seeds which will bear that fruit.

Today we are asked to lead better lives, to be good people. "Thou shall not lie," "Thou shall not kill," "Thou shall not be selfish." Live up to those commandments. Tomorrow will take care of itself. Worrying about it is only a waste. Who knows, there may not even be a tomorrow, and then what will all that worry have gained? People worry about 1990. Are you sure there will be a 1990? Positively? Today you are sure you are here, so why not enjoy today? Although all the scriptures have said something about the future, we do not need to go into those things. There are so many things they have asked us to do now; let us do them.

Do not expect anything to be eternal. The only thing that is eternal is the consciousness. The consciousness is there in everything, even in an atom. Leave tomorrow to God, the cosmic power that created everything. If He has assigned you to take care of something, go, do it. If not, why worry about it. "It is Your business, Lord. You created me, You created all the other characters, and when You want to end the play, You will finish it." That is how we should feel. He is the one who is playing with all these things. We are all pawns in His hands. So we should just enjoy the game.

I do not think that the end of the world is at hand. It is going to stay many, many thousands of years more. We can sleep safely. Nothing will fall down. There is no particular reason for me to say so, I just feel that it is true. If you insisted that I give a reason, probably I would say that I see more and more people becoming better people, becoming good, wanting to know the truth. Why are all these young people taking such an interest in bettering the world? They could be spending their time in movies, concerts, nightclubs. Why should they even be questioning everything? The consciousness of the people is changing and they want to know more of the truth, they want to learn how to lead better lives.

Very often they ask me, "How can the world be saved?" My answer is, first of all by saving yourself; you are a part of the world. Unless and until you do that, you are in no condition to save the rest of the world. Save yourself first, and then save everyone else. Like charity, it begins at home. In a way the outside world is your own making. You create your world. If you are good, the whole world will be good.

To make the world right, each individual should be easeful, peaceful and useful. Find ease and peace in your life, and then others will find a use for you. Think that you are a nice instrument, ready to be used for the good of all. If an instrument wants to perform an operation safely, what should it do? It should first of all get itself sterilized, right? Free itself from any dangerous viruses, bacteria. Only then is it fit to operate. In the same way, if you want to go and operate on the cancer in the world, you had better become sterilized. Soak yourself in spirit. That is what you call "spirituality." Get rid of all the undesirable things that could worsen the problem. Go as a clean instrument. Then you can really be instrumental in saving the world.

Sometimes people say, "Oh, Swami, where is the time for all that? I have too much cleaning to do. By the time I get myself completely pure there may not even be a world." Don't worry. Take care of first things first. If you don't have time to do both the inner work and outer work, just concentrate on the inner cleaning for now. Why? If you do not, you are just going to be spreading poison. If there is no time to clean the instrument, it should just sit in the closet and not even go near the operating room. That would be the most useful thing for it to do.

We do not have to look forward to a new age; it is already here. If the vision of the new age is to see more and more people living peacefully, living harmoniously, living lovingly, we are already seeing it. More spiritual communities are cropping up, more self-help groups. People are realizing that they cannot help anyone else until they help themselves, and they are recognizing that they are part of one universal family. It is happening all over. People want to forget the superficial differences and live together, caring and sharing. This is just the beginning.

Imagine that you have a huge pile of apples, and you want to change the entire heap into oranges. How would you do it? There is only one way. Take out one apple, put in one orange; take out another apple, put in another orange. One by one, one by one.

You are also a part of this insane world, are you not? In order to correct the world, you must first correct yourself, so that at least that one small part is peaceful. Inspire the next one by your example. If, by watching you, someone else becomes a little sane, then at least there are two sane people. Two can inspire a third. Don't we even clean up our neighborhoods that way? It is called "Fix Up, Paint Up" week. Each family cleans up its own yard, the piece of sidewalk in front of its own house, and when they are all done, the entire neighborhood is clean. It is not that one person tried to clean the whole neighborhood by herself. Each one just takes care of its own, and the whole becomes clean.

It is the same thing with making the world peaceful. Imagine a huge room full of people with everyone talking at once. They are all gossiping, whispering to each other. All of a sudden they all realize that there is too much noise. Immediately everybody says, "Hey, come on, stop that noise! Let's be quiet! Hey, I say be silent!" All at the same time, everybody shouts, "Keep quiet, people!" "I want silence!" Each one says something. Is there silence? In the name of silence they are shouting. The only way to find at least one corner of the room silent is to shut your own mouth. If each one did that, the goal would be achieved.

If we would enlarge our thinking, if we would go beyond the "mine" and "ours" that limit us, that would really help the world avoid all these calamities. Now is the time. Disarmament conferences are going on everywhere. If we cannot do it today, we are not going to have another opportunity. That will be the end. If a war comes there will be no winner and no loser. There will simply be nobody at all. By our wrong thinking we have brought the world to this level. But that terrible outcome can be averted. It is still in our hands. Spend more time in prayer, send your good wishes to everybody. Prove that you love everybody.

Instead of thinking about enemies and planning for war, why don't we stretch out a friendly hand and say, "Forget about all this arguing. I am tired of it; I am sure you are also tired of all these things. Your people want to be peaceful. Our people also want to be peaceful. We have no intention of destroying you. We have no desire to destroy you."

The public is really getting tired of the politicians' peace talks. The more the politicians talk about peace for the whole world, the more the world falls to pieces. How many peace talks have there been? Not even one brought any lasting result. I think it is time for the public to take this matter into their own hands. Write letters to the Soviet Union. Not to the Premier, to anybody. "Anybody in the Soviet Union, I am an American. I love you all. I don't want to hate you anymore." "Postmaster General, please send this to anybody in the country."

Why not? Perhaps you don't agree with their way of government or the actions of that government. Fine. Just because you are friendly with someone doesn't mean that you accept everything that person does. Sometimes you even have disagreements with your friends, is it not so?

What do you think the Soviet Union is? It is not a big monster ready to gobble us up. It is people. Families, innocent little babies, sweet children, young people who sing and dance, mothers and fathers who love and support their children. Career people: artists, musicians, athletes, doctors, accountants, farmers, teachers, plumbers, computer programmers. They are just like us. We should let the public know that it is the politicians, the leaders, who are frightened and mistrusting. We see the people as just like us, we love them. We want to be friends. They have nothing to fear from us. We don't want to take them over; we can even learn from each other. No ideology has worked one hundred percent. The communists could learn something from us, and we could even learn something from them. Without fear, there will be no hatred; and without hatred, there will be peace everywhere.

World Leaders

A truly religious leader—a person who believes in a faith or in God—would never want to see or cause any kind of violence in any form. He or she would feel that all people are the representations of God—no matter to what country, what color, what caste or what creed they belong.

We should select leaders who are totally neutral, impartial people, people who would think of the entire country, who have renounced a personal life to serve the country. It is not easy to be a leader. Once elected as the top officer of a country, one does not belong to any particular group, but to everyone, even to the whole world. It is hard to find such leaders now. That is why every country is in trouble today.

At least we should be learning a good lesson from all these things. Do not elect a person because you belong to the same party. Forget all about parties. Is he a sane person? Will she see that justice is done? Will he serve without any personal motives behind his actions? Select leaders like that, good-hearted neutral people, saintly people, sane people. They should be people who will honestly say, "I am a servant of the people. That is all I know." It is hard to find neutral people without any personal motives behind their actions; but until we do, we are going to continue facing these problems. So be careful when the next election comes.

Suspicion has ruined many, many lives, and now it is ruining our world. Most of our human problems, whether they are in individuals or communities or even nations, arise from suspicion.

I had the good fortune of hearing and seeing Gandhiji several times when I was much younger. Many of my close relatives were involved in his movement, so in that way I knew him very well. The recent movie has really done a very good job of presenting him properly. There was no exaggeration at all. If there is any criticism I could make in that regard, it would be that there was much more to his life and work that was left out of the film. Of course, they could not put everything in, but there were so many more wonderful parts of his life.

Although the Indians might claim him as "our Gandhi," "an Indian," he did not consider himself to be an Indian. He was a world citizen. His philosophy is good for anybody and everybody. The real Gandhiji was immortal spirit, and in that sense he will always be alive. Even in the physical world, his memory, his work, his influence is so widespread and so great that it really is not accurate to speak of him in the past tense.

His philosophy is very much alive, although there are still many people who are not yet convinced that non-violence is a better way than violence. But history is the proof of that; with his philosophy he was able to regain independence for India from a very powerful regime without so much as raising his arm. I think the movie "Gandhi" came to America at just the right time. There are a lot of radicals around saying, "We have to destroy the other side, we have to stop this threat." It is time for them to learn from this movie that if you really want an arms freeze, your own arm should be frozen. You should not even raise a fist and shout. Gandhiji did not merely teach people how to act, but also how to love, how to be peaceful even in the midst of violence. They put their faith in God, the soul force, not in the physical force or weapon force. With that simple, humble, loving tactic, he liberated the whole of India from one of the greatest political powers the world has ever known. The time for us to heed this great lesson is long overdue. Let all the leaders of the world live in love and truth. It is time for us to trust in God that way and to do the right thing.

Spiritual Understanding

We all have unity, and at the same time, diversity. Physically, mentally and materially we are all different. We do not think the same way. Although we sometimes say we are thinking alike, our thoughts are never one hundred percent the same. Even when we gather for a common purpose our thoughts are still different. No mind is exactly the same as another mind. Nature never makes duplicates. Scientists say that not even two snowflakes are exactly alike. There is constant variety in creation. Mentally we are different; physically we are different. The only thing in which we are not different is our awareness, our consciousness, the light within – or, as the Bible calls it, the image of God. In that we are all one. The same light is shining through many different colored lamps.

That diversity is necessary because we all have to play different parts in this cosmic drama. Each one comes into the drama with different makeup and costumes. Unfortunately we do not make up our minds to live up to the truth that we are really all one behind the costumes. That is the reason there is so much chaos in this world right now, even in the religious field. As many of you certainly know, more lives have been lost in the name of God and religion than for any other reason. All the political wars and natural calamities together have not killed as many people.

This shows that there is something terribly wrong in our approach. We are looking at the superficial side of religion and forgetting to go deep into its foundation. If we did, we would find that all the religions ultimately talk about the same God, the same Truth;

but somehow we ignore that common base and continue to fight over the superficial aspects. It is time for us to recognize that Truth is one, there cannot be two truths. If we would only realize that, we could enjoy the variety in our expression of that Truth. Variety is the spice of life, no doubt. We need it for enjoyment. If we were all the same—looked the same, thought the same—I think this world would be a very boring place. The varieties add charm to our life.

Think about food for a minute. Each person likes something different. But even though our tastes may differ, we would not deny other people because of that. We do not cast them aside: "You are bread and butter people. Go away! I like salad. Everybody should eat salad. Anyone who eats something else is wrong." Fortunately—so far at least—we have not started separating people in the name of food. We know that there is only one purpose for eating, though we may eat many foods, and that is to satisfy our hunger. This is an excellent example of the unity in purpose and the variety in expression.

Life should be like that. When we forget that unity, the variety is not fun anymore. It becomes a basis for fighting. If we could remember that unity always, we would find real peace, harmony, and joy in this world. There is nothing else to be done. It is the lack of this understanding that has created all the wars and the crisis that we are in now. Mere scientific discovery is not to blame. The scientists themselves are not to blame. The fault is in the way we use the scientific discoveries.

There is nothing wrong with atomic energy, nuclear energy. We just use it in the wrong way. I would ask you, is a knife good or bad? Cut a fruit, the knife is good. Cut a finger, the knife is bad. What about fire, is it good or bad? If you sit close to it, you feel warm. If you sit too close to it, you get burned. So what would you say, are these things good or bad? We are the ones who determine that. If we are good, everything is good; if we are bad, we make use of everything for bad purposes. All these wars are created by human minds that seem to lack the proper understanding. My sincere wish and prayer is that one day we will all realize our essential oneness, enjoy our differences and live together as one universal family.

That is why we are building the Light Of Truth Universal Shrine (LOTUS). It is one shrine dedicated to the light of all faiths, and to world peace. I am finding that the LOTUS project is very much appreciated by everyone, everywhere I go. I tell them clearly, "If we want to put an end to all these worldly problems, whatever they are, we should go to the very root. The root cause for all this disharmony is the lack of spiritual understanding." It is from ignorance of our spiritual oneness that we commit crimes, deny each other, kill each other, rob each other.

Take, for example, the racial problems that we are facing today. Wherever you go, you see a problem between blacks and whites. In some places, people are killing each other. Why? Because our understanding has not gone beyond a fraction of a millimeter of skin. The color is just on the surface of the skin; it does not even permeate the entire skin. If you simply scratch both, what do you get? Neither white nor black, but red. See how superficial our vision is? How different our lives would be if we would only realize that all of us function by the same spirit. The body is nothing but a vehicle. "She has a black car; I have a white car."

Look at poverty. Why are there poor people? Because there are so many rich people. It is just nature's law. In order for one fellow to become a multi-millionaire, at least a hundred people have to become total paupers. Otherwise, how can one person become rich? If one country wastes food, ten other countries starve. Do you think just by feeding the starving people you will put an end to starvation? Not at all. The reason for starvation is not the lack of food. The world census says that we are about four and a half billion people on the surface of this earth. Do you know that the world agricultural statistics say we are growing food enough for twelve billion people? So we have almost three times more food than we actually need. Why should anybody be starving then? If the statistics are correct, there is no reason for anyone to starve. Then what is the reason for starvation? We don't share, we don't care. Tons of food are dumped into the sea just to keep prices under control.

Of course we send a lot of food and aid. We do many things to help, but there is much more that could be done if we were only more generous. If we would say about all the people in all the countries, "They are my brothers and sisters," we would want to do much more than we are doing now.

The cause of hunger is the lack of spiritual understanding, and the solution is to see the same spirit in everyone. The same is true of all the crimes, whatever problem you look at. If I love you as my own Self, will I sell cigarettes and pollute your lungs just to get your money in my pocket? If there was this kind of love in the world, would we see so much pornography? Even young children are not spared. Why? For what? For money. Is it not so? Just for the sake of money people sell their conscience, their own innocent children. It is such a shame.

The root of all these problems is this lack of spiritual understanding. That is why, whatever we do to treat these problems will bring only temporary results. We can only eradicate the problem completely if we go to the very root of it and treat the cause. That is where religion comes in. Our religious education should bring us together, make us feel that we are one family, a world family. No matter what you are, where you are, what your faith is, you are my brother, my sister.

That is the purpose of LOTUS. That is why even the least little bit of energy that you put into projects like this will go a long way to make the world a better place. If you like to help other good causes, wonderful; do it. But do not stop with temporary results. This message seems to be appreciated by one and all now. Everywhere, everywhere. Many have changed their hearts.

This LOTUS is only a beginning. I know that once people see the beauty and the benefit of it, every city and town will want a LOTUS. Every religion can have its own church or temple, and that is fine; but this shrine will be one place where everybody—all believers, and even non-believers—will be able to come and meet together. I am sure that all the towns will have such a place one day. This kind of universal shrine doesn't belong to only one organization, but it has to begin somewhere. Probably God has chosen us as instruments to do that.

Our aim is to educate people: "Let us not fight in the name of religion. Let us know that we are all one in spirit." The moment that kind of understanding comes (the realization that we are all essentially one in spirit, although we appear as many), all of our physical and material problems will be solved. Until then, the problems will continue. Once you know that the other person is your own Self, you will not see him as black or white. You won't see her as being any different from yourself. You won't need to go and rob his pocket. You won't have any reason to start a fight. All of the crimes will be eliminated, because the cause of crime will be eliminated. There will be no "yours" and "mine"; no separation, no jealousy, no hatred.

There is no shortcut to this end. We have been trying to solve our problems in many different ways, but we have not tried to treat the basic cause. Now the time is right. We are slowly beginning to understand the cause for all our health problems, and we are slowly beginning to change our eating and living habits. We are trying to eliminate all the poisons that come into our systems. More and more people have stopped smoking. More and more people have stopped taking meat, refined sugar, alcohol. Why? Because everyone is becoming aware that so many of our physical diseases and mental difficulties stem from wrong living and wrong eating.

In the same way, until and unless the basic cause for all our world problems is eliminated, all the relief our solutions bring will be temporary. It is like painkillers. You may have killed the pain, but you have not rooted out the cause. If you have weeds in your garden do you simply pluck the stems and the leaves? No, you dig deep and take them up by the roots. Otherwise they just keep coming back. If the root cause is there, the problem will still return.

And the root cause is that we do not see our own spirit. We are all one spiritual family, and we should all be taking care of each other. Anything that is done to bring this kind of understanding, to bring this knowledge to people, is the greatest charity. There are charities which put food on tables today, and I am very happy about that. They perform a great service. But it is important to eliminate the *cause* of starvation, not just feed the starving. If we eliminate the cause, there will no longer be starving people to feed.

Let us come forward to make this a reality. I am not talking just about the LOTUS, I am talking about making this understanding a reality. Wherever you go, talk to people. Tell them, "We may look different, but we are all one in spirit. Hello, my brother. Hello, my sister." Care and share, love and give. Apply it in your own life. Then you are carrying a LOTUS in your heart. And that LOTUS light will shine within and without. Please let us all do our share. Nobody is insignificant. Everybody, even a little child can do something. Let all the minds think in these terms and come forward to do something so that the entire creation may be filled with Peace and Joy, Love and Light. OM *Shanthi*. Thank you.

Appendix

Index

Rev. Sri Swami Satchidananda

The Reverend Sri Swami Satchidananda is a world renowned spiritual leader and Yoga Master. He himself is a living example of both the teachings of Yoga—which are those same ethical foundation stones upon which all religions are based—and its goal: leading an easeful, peaceful, useful life. Not limited to any one organization, religion or country, Sri Swamiji receives invitations from around the world to lecture and serve as advisor to international Yoga and ecumenical organizations. These invitations have taken him throughout the United States, Canada, Europe, Australia, India and Sri Lanka, and to South America, New Zealand, Japan, Hong Kong, Malaysia, China and the Soviet Union. He has dedicated his life to the cause of peace—both individual and universal—and to religious harmony among all people. The Light Of Truth Universal Shrine (LOTUS) will be an embodiment of that peace, and a place for all to come and experience it for themselves.